ON OUR OWN TERMS

CHILDREN LIVING WITH PHYSICAL DISABILITIES

DON'T
TURN
AWAY

Library of Congress Cataloging-in-Publication Data

Bergman, Thomas, 1947-
    On our own terms.

    (Don't turn away)
    Translation of: Varför blunda!
    Summary: Describes the activities at the Caroline Hospital in Stockholm where children with congenital handicaps receive training and physiotherapy.
        1. Physically handicapped children--Juvenile literature. [1. Physically handicapped]
I. Title. II. Series: Bergman, Thomas, 1947-   . Don't turn away.
HV903.B4613   1988   362.1'088054   88-42973
ISBN 1-55532-942-X

D O N 'T
T U R N
A W A Y

North American edition first published in 1989 by

Gareth Stevens, Inc.
7317 West Green Tree Road
Milwaukee, Wisconsin 53223, USA

First published in Swedish by Cikada under the title *Varför blunda!*

Series Editor: MaryLee Knowlton
Research Editor: Scott Enk
Series Designer: Kate Kriege

Printed in the United States of America

1 2 3 4 5 6 7 8 9 95 94 93 92 91 90 89

ON OUR OWN TERMS

CHILDREN LIVING WITH PHYSICAL DISABILITIES

DON'T
TURN
AWAY

Thomas Bergman

Gareth Stevens Children's Books
MILWAUKEE

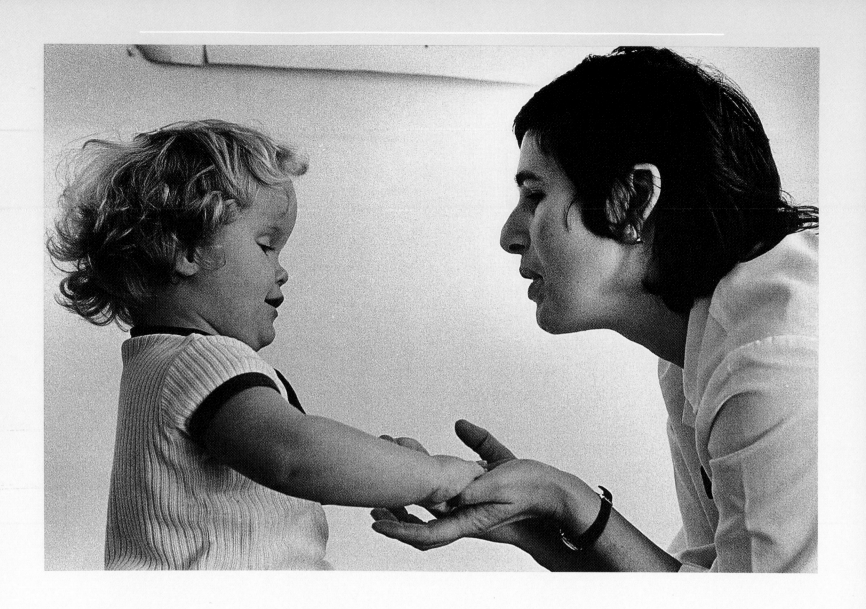

When Thomas Bergman first showed me the remarkable photographs that appear in On Our Own Terms, I was struck by their power to capture the essence of children's personalities and moods. As we looked at them together — I for the first time, he once again after many times — I was moved by the intensity and passion of a person who cares deeply about children who have physical disabilities.

Thomas is Sweden's best-known children's photographer, with a reputation stretching from Europe to Japan. His compassion, admiration, and affection for children with disabilities inspired him to embark on a special photographic mission. The striking black-and-white photographs you will see in this book will remain in your memory. The thoughts and feelings that Thomas' young friends have shared with him form the basis for the insightful text that accompanies the pictures.

You will meet children in the pages of this book with disabilities that may be unfamiliar to you. You will be inspired by the originality and courage with which they meet the challenges presented by these disabilities. And you will be moved by the many ways that they are like children everywhere. I hope you will ask yourself, as I did, "Why haven't I met many children like these? Where are they? Why don't I see them in the schools and on playgrounds, in museums and shopping malls, on the streets and in the parks?" These are the questions we must explore. Our communities should embrace all people. We will _all_ be the richer for it.

In On Our Own Terms, Helena, Carina, Annelie, Patrick, and many other courageous children show us that a disability should not be a cause for separation, embarrassment, and fear. Instead, it should be a reason for reaching out, sharing the joys, sorrows, and hopes of our lives.

Gareth Stevens
Gareth Stevens
PUBLISHER

Many children are born each year with physical disabilities. Others become disabled through illness or accident. The Karolinska Hospital in Stockholm, Sweden, has a clinic for the treatment of children with physical disabilities that restrict or impair their movement.

Not too many years ago, the families and doctors of children like these would have been satisfied to keep the children healthy. The children would have been confined to wheelchairs, sometimes in institutions. People felt that the most important goal for children who had already suffered was to avoid more suffering. So they made their decisions for them, took care of them, and eliminated their need to work or think. Things have changed.

Today we recognize that people with disabilities need what everyone else needs — the chance to develop in every way to the best of his or her abilities. Respect for what people can do has taken the place of pity for what they cannot do.

The children who come to the clinic at the Karolinska Hospital come to work. Some come each day or several times a week for physical therapy. Some stay for weeks at a time for intensive treatment and monitoring. The therapists and staff doctors, together with the parents and children, if they are old enough, develop an individual treatment plan for each child. The plan specifies goals for the treatment and ways of working toward the goals, both at the clinic and at home.

In the pages that follow, you will meet some of the children who come to the clinic to work. You will also meet the therapists who work with them.

Thomas Bergman

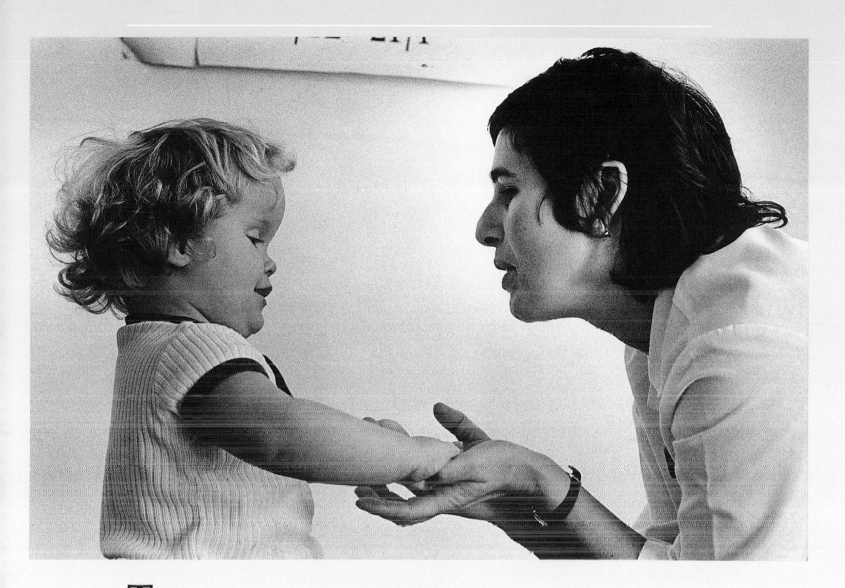

This is Kicki, who just turned three. Right now, Kicki can only walk if someone holds her up, because the lower half of her body is paralyzed. She and her therapist, Christina, are working to develop the strength in her arms and her back. They work with mirrors both in front of them and behind so Kicki can see exactly how she looks when she sits well. She wants to walk with a walker or crutches. Kicki is very determined. Looking at herself in a mirror, she says, "Kicki is strong. Kicki wants to." Christina knows that Kicki's determination will help her get up on her feet.

Kicki was born with spina bifida, which means "divided spine." Spina bifida is an inherited condition that in Kicki's case has resulted in total paralysis of her legs and a dislocated hip. She has no feeling below her waist.

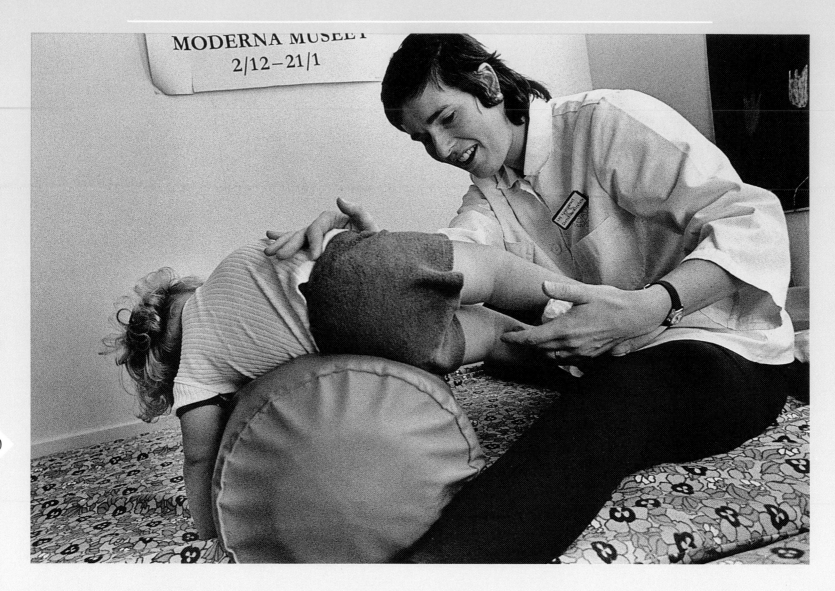

Today Kicki and Christina are working on the big roller. They are trying to train her hip to move in a more useful way. Later Christina seats Kicki on the roller and they play horsie. It looks like fun, and it is, but they're really working to improve Kicki's balance.

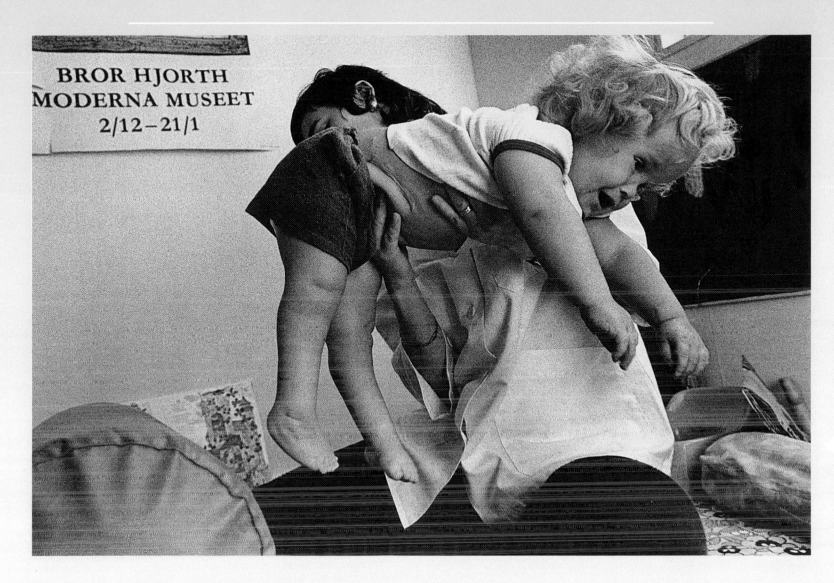

By the end of the session, Kicki is tired. Christina has to coax and promise rewards to get the little girl to work. Kicki's body was not designed to do what she and Christina are trying to teach it.

Because Kicki has no feeling or strength in the lower part of her body, she cannot tell when she has to go to the bathroom and must have help.

Bjorn is nine years old and has been coming to the clinic for several years. He and his therapist, Britta, have been working together for a long time. Bjorn has cerebral palsy. "Cerebral" means the condition is centered in the brain, and "palsy" means paralysis or muscle weakness. It is among the most common birth defects. It can also be caused during or after birth by an injury to the head.

Bjorn cannot sit by himself and he has trouble holding his head straight and still. In therapy, he and Britta sit on a large roller in front of a mirror. Looking into the mirror, Bjorn tries to find a good sitting position and to keep his head straight.

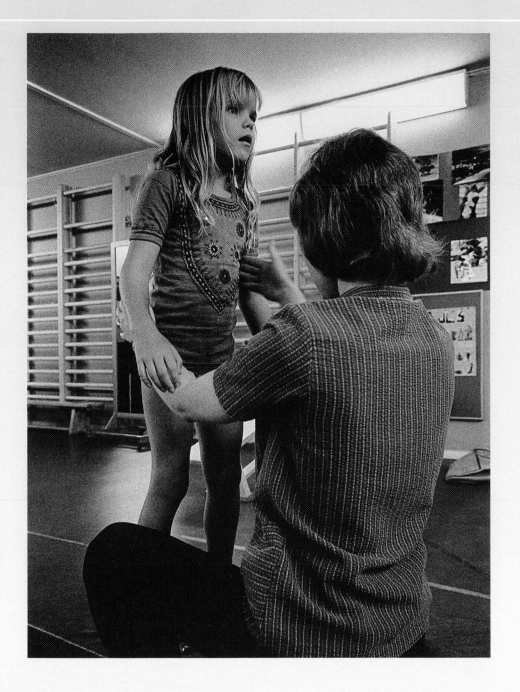

Annelie is nine years old. About a year ago, she was badly hurt in a car accident. Her spine was damaged and she was unconscious for five months. She is only now beginning to leave her wheelchair and learn to walk again.

Annelie is unsure if her legs will hold her. In the past, she has found them too weak and has fallen. Today, the long months of therapy seem to be paying off. Carefully, she goes on to step over small sandbags with her therapist's support.

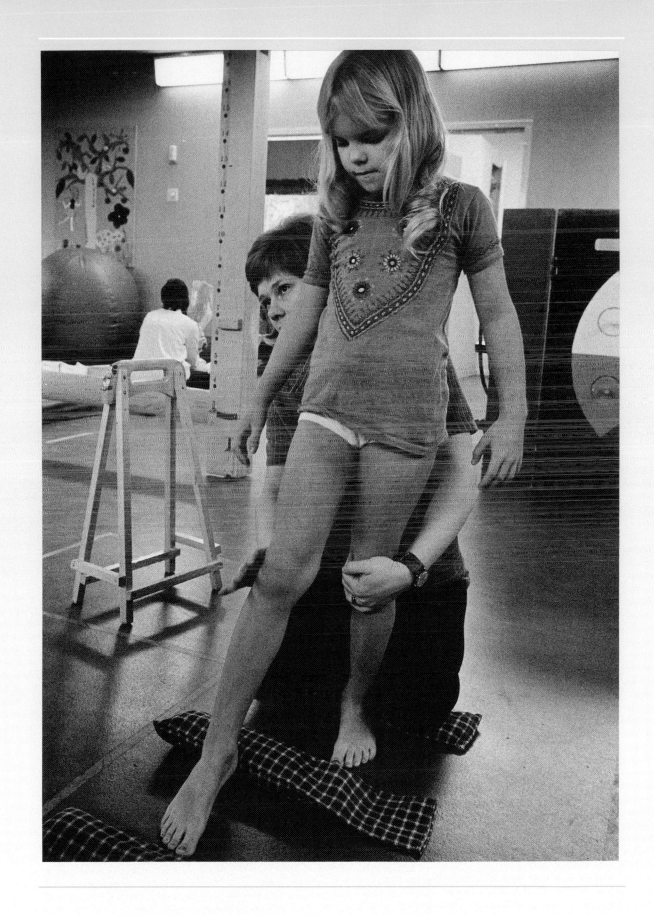

Annelie and Kerstin, her therapist, are very fond of each other. Annelie knows that Kerstin's prodding will help her. They both believe that Annelie will recover completely from her injuries.

The physical therapists at Karolinska Hospital are well educated and experienced. They know how to evaluate the condition of a child's body and the possibilities for growth and development. They can devise appropriate therapy goals and programs.

But they all know that their technical skills are only a part of the reason for their success. Equally important is their ability to motivate their small clients. The affection and respect the children and therapists feel for each other get them through some sad, painful, and discouraging days. Although to an outsider, much of the therapy looks like ordinary play, it is tiring and often painful work. As the children learn to do things they have never done before, they must often unlearn ways they have protected themselves. Their safe, protected ways are replaced with risky, new ways. They need to be able to trust their therapist, their guide.

17

Another therapist, Sabine, reads a story to two-year-old Liv, who, like Bjorn, was born with cerebral palsy. Liv cannot sit or walk by herself, but Sabine and the story help her to sit and to hold her head up. Liv loves to be read to and, as you can see, a storybook can be good physical therapy.

19

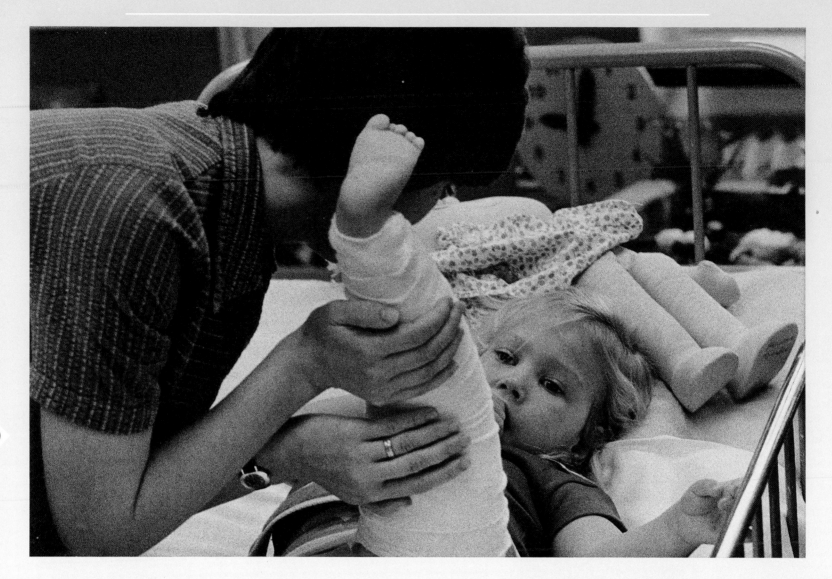

Six-year-old Helena has spina bifida. Her legs are not completely paralyzed, but are not very strong. Unless she uses them, the muscles will weaken and the bones will become very brittle. Helena has no feeling in her legs, so several months ago, when she broke her leg, she did not feel any pain. Children with spina bifida are taught to check their skin for irritations and injuries since they often do not feel heat, cold, pain, or pressure.

Since she broke her leg, Helena has had to wear a cast and not put any weight on it. Her therapist, Agneta, helps her to move her legs so that her hips and legs don't become stiff. When the cast comes off, Helena wants to be able to walk again with crutches.

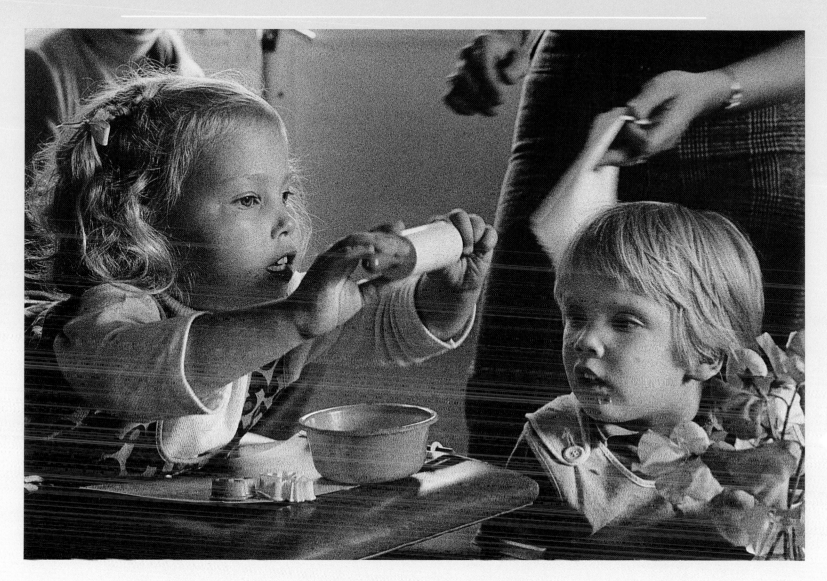

Helena's best friend at the clinic is Dan. Dan has spina bifida, too. Helena has been staying at the hospital since she broke her leg and each morning she looks forward to seeing Dan, who comes in the morning. Today they are making cookies in the playroom. The children don't even notice that the cookie making is therapy — reaching, rolling, gripping tightly.

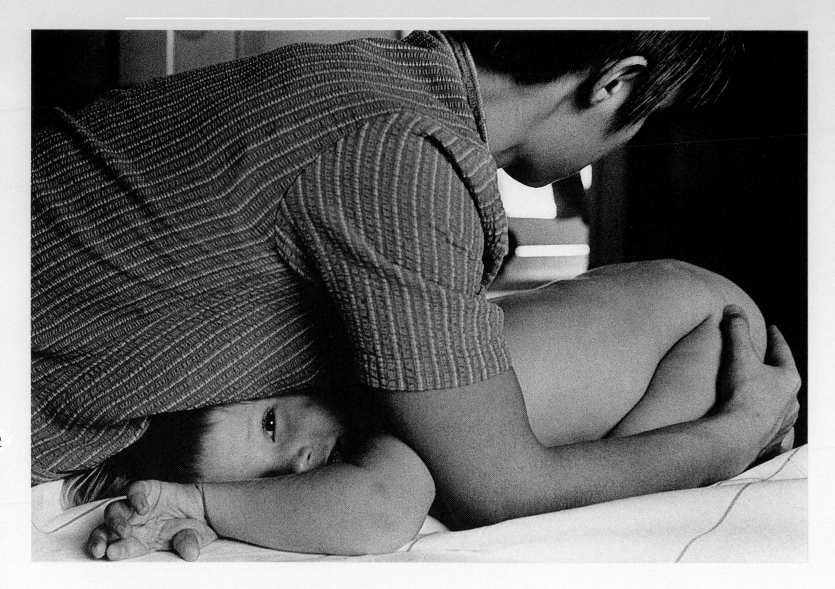

Dan knows this is therapy, though. It's hard work. His therapist, Lotte, holds him tightly. Dan's job is to push hard against her to strengthen his muscles. He's tempted just to lie peacefully in this comfortable position, but Lotte encourages him to push up as she pushes down.

While Helena waits for Dan to finish his therapy, she tours the corridors of the clinic. She has a little turtle on wheels. She lies on her tummy and sort of dog-paddles on the floor with her hands. By the time she has visited all the other children, maybe Dan will be finished. If he's not, she'll go around again. Traveling on her turtle strengthens Helena's back and arms and encourages her to keep her head up. Besides being good therapy, it's also great fun.

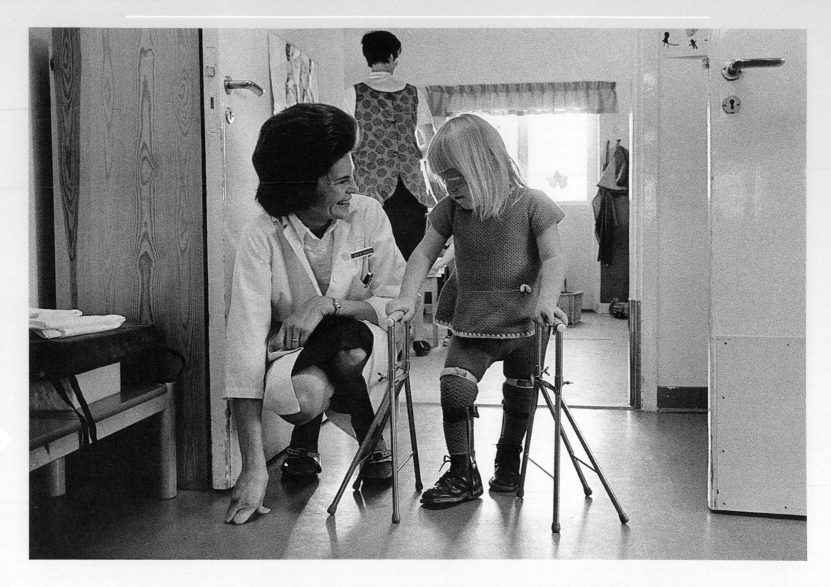

Coming down the hall is Ingela. Ingela also has spina bifida. After years of hard work and therapy, Ingela can walk quite a long way supported by braces and crutches. She is a bright child with a good chance for a full life.

Here is Ronny, born three years ago without arms or legs. He needed loads of help and training to learn how to do almost everything. But his spirit was strong and when a way to do something occurred to him, he threw himself into it — really! Since he couldn't walk, he taught himself to get around by rolling across the floor.

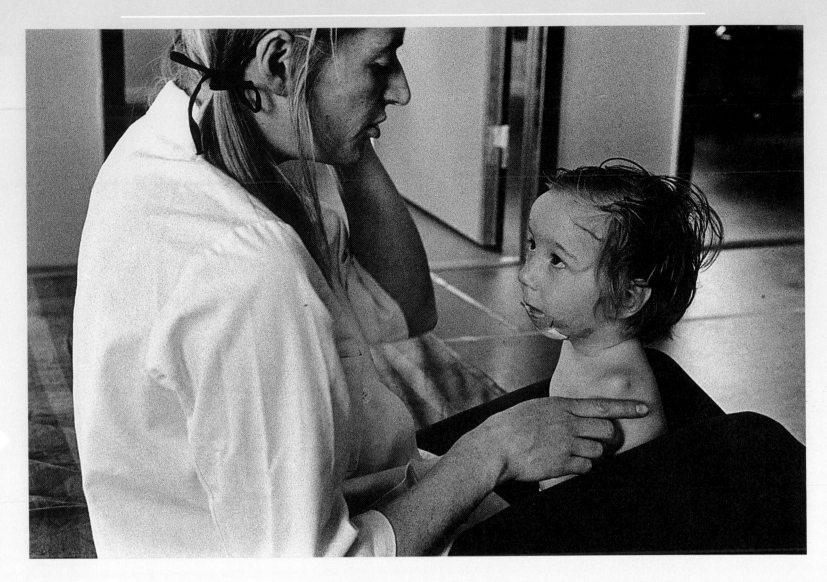

Ronny also learned to pick things up with his right foot and with his mouth. Here he and his therapist, Mia, are shown working on his sitting. This was hard for Ronny because without arms he could not soften the landing when he tipped over and he often hurt his face. But between Mia's knees or on a soft rug, he was not afraid.

With his feet, Ronny had to do many things other people do with their hands. His therapy program included this exercise to strengthen his toes and increase their coordination so he could pick up toys and other things with his feet.

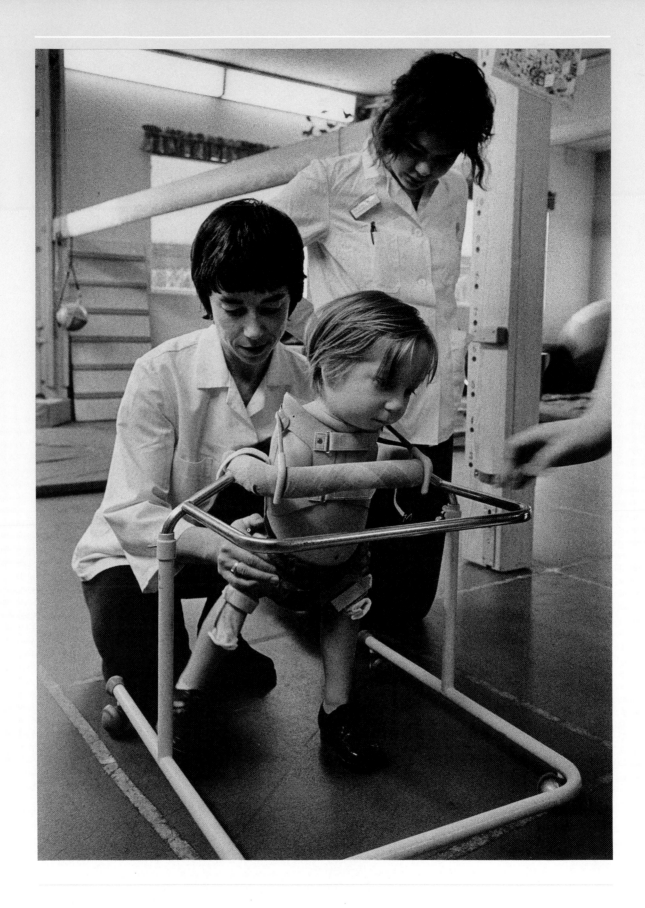

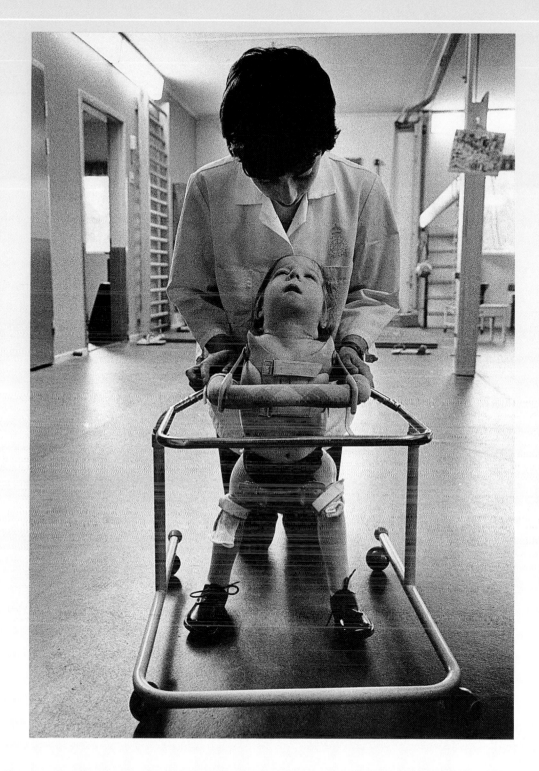

Walking on his new artificial legs and supporting himself with his new artificial arms was strange for Ronny, and he did not like it much. Walking from one end of the room to the other was very tiring. Looking down into his pleading eyes, the therapist understood. Enough for today.

Time to eat. Even mealtime is therapy, a chance to teach children skills they need to make them as independent as possible.

The clinic made a special spoon for Ronny so he could feed himself. When he turned his head the spoon went down. When he lowered his head, the spoon came up to his mouth with food. A nurse was always nearby if he needed help.

Seated in a box that kept him feeling secure and safe from falls, Ronny watched the other children at the clinic. After a rest, he would roll around the floor after them.

Sometimes the weaknesses of a child's body go beyond what you can see in a picture. Since these pictures were taken, Ronny died from an infection that his body could not fight.

Anne was born with shortened arms and only one finger on each hand. With her friend Marie, she has a tea party with water. She doesn't do things the same way that children with normal arms and hands do, but she does many things just as well in her own way. She can draw, she can paint, and she can dress herself even with buttons and zippers.

33

With a grin and a quick movement, Anne has played one of her favorite tricks on a volunteer. Pretending to hold hands, she slips a watch off the volunteer's arm and onto her own. Anne knows how to have fun!

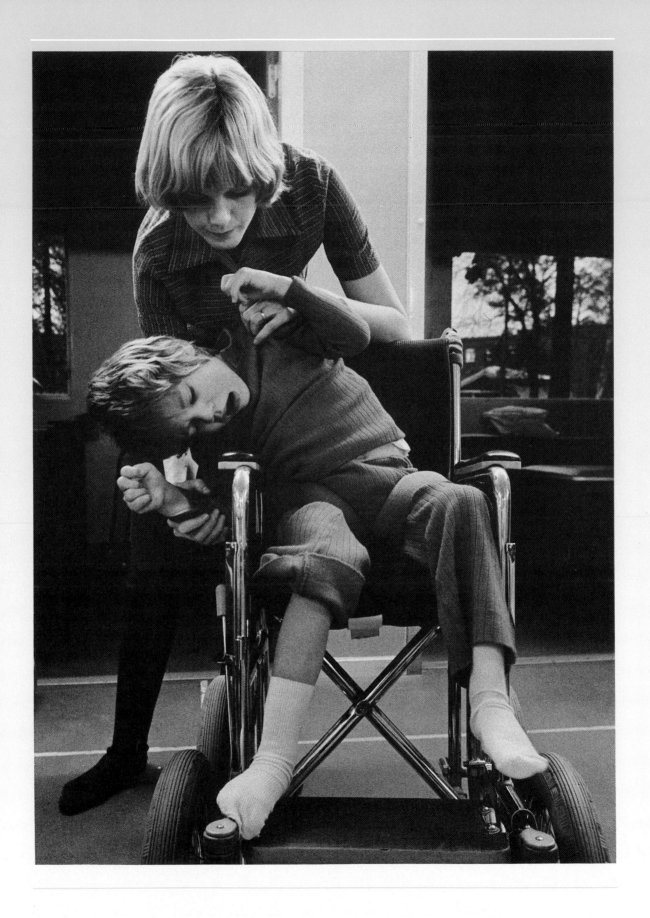

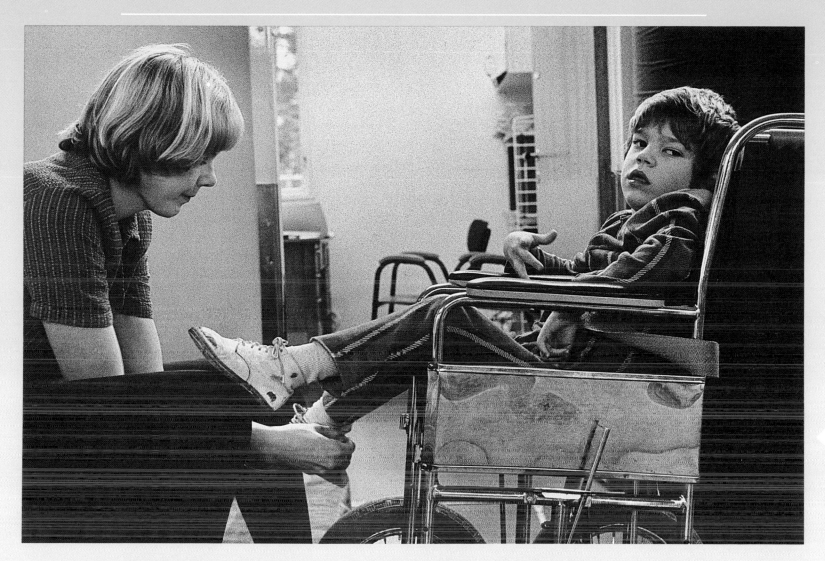

Eight-year-old Carina has had severe brain damage. She is unable to control her movements, so she is fastened into her wheelchair with a safety belt so she doesn't fall. Her therapist, Karin, works with her twice a day. They have just finished training on the rug, and Carina relaxes after being helped back into her chair.

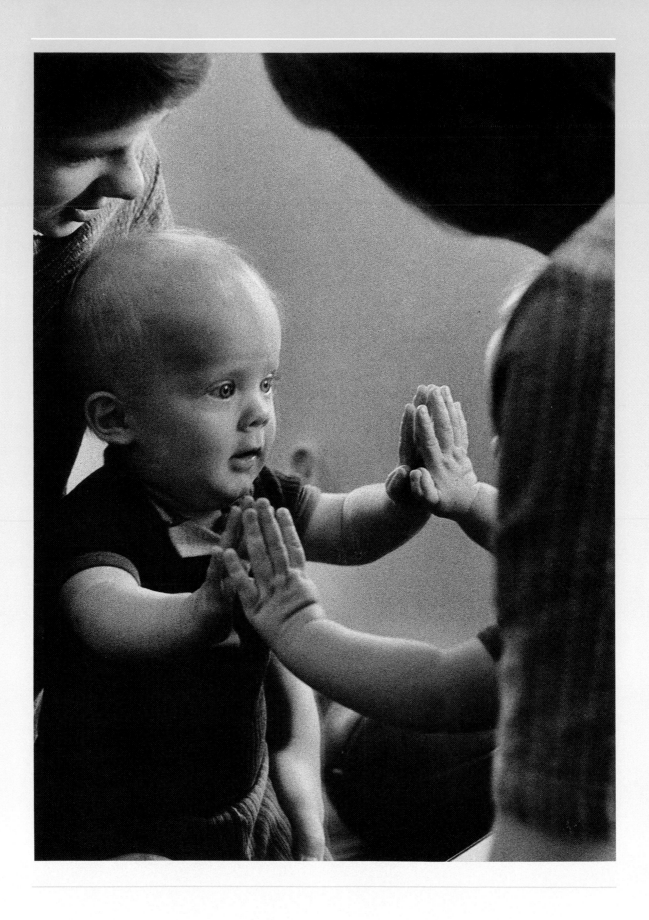

Patrick is just ten months old. He has slight brain damage that has affected his movements. His leg muscles are very tense and not well controlled. With Kerstin supporting his legs, Patrick is learning how to stand the right way. Getting therapy this young, at the same age a normal child would learn to stand, is important for Patrick. If he learns to do things the right, hard way, he won't have to unlearn bad habits. Working at the mirror is fun. Babies like to look at themselves anyway, and Patrick can see himself standing right.

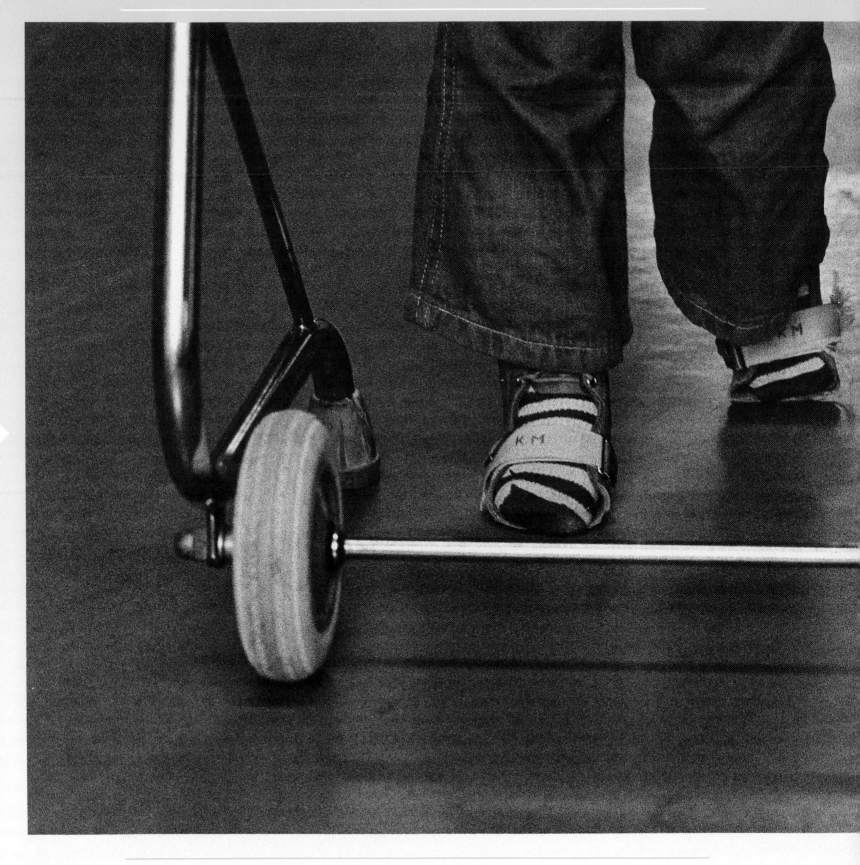

Two little feet come down the corridor. The braces and the roller help now. Some day, these feet might run without them. Maybe not. But with or without devices, this child has somewhere to go.

At the end of a session, the end of a day, therapists and clients become just adults and children. The effort they've shared and the closeness they feel is apparent in their comfort with each other.

QUESTIONS FROM CHILDREN ABOUT PHYSICAL DISABILITIES

Having questions in your mind can keep you from feeling comfortable with people whose abilities are different from yours. Here are some answers to questions we have all asked ourselves.

What does it mean to say that someone has a physical disability?

Having a physical disability restricts the way people can move their bodies. Some people with physical disabilities cannot walk well and some cannot walk at all. Some people cannot move any part of their body. Some people cannot control the movements of their muscles.

Some physical disabilities are caused by injuries or diseases. Others are caused by things that happen before birth. Physical disabilities can result from damage to a person's body or to the brain.

How can brain damage affect what the body can do?

You probably already know that your brain makes it possible for you to think. But it does more than that. It also controls everything your body does, even when you're not thinking about it. It sends messages to every part of your body to tell it what to do. If the brain is damaged, it may not be able to communicate well with the other parts of the body. Then the body will not do everything it is supposed to do.

Brain damage can impair a person's ability to think, move, see, or hear. In most cases, it cannot be corrected or cured.

Teachers and therapists who work with brain-damaged children try hard to find out just what each child can do. This is important because some types of damage can hide other skills that a person might have. For example, people who cannot talk at all or move very much may have artistic or musical talents or brilliant minds. People who work with these children try to help them develop all their abilities so they won't be limited by their disabilities.

What causes brain damage?

Some brain damage is caused by diseases. Some is caused by injuries before or during birth. Some is caused by injuries after birth. Doctors do not always know the causes of brain damage. But some brain damage can be prevented. You should know that babies and children who are dropped or beaten can suffer brain damage. If you or someone you know is being abused in this way, talk to a teacher or other grown-up you trust. Your brain — or anyone else's — is too important to risk.

Are "spastic" and "cripple" bad words?

The word "spastic" comes from the word "spasm." Both words refer to a sudden muscle contraction that the person cannot control. If that's what you mean when you use the word, it's not a bad word. Most often a person with a spastic condition has cerebral palsy. Cerebral palsy is a condition that causes spastic movements, or spasticity.

When you use "spastic" as a name for a person who has spastic movements or for a friend or classmate who is bothering you, you are misusing the word. You will make disabled people and those who care about them feel uncomfortable and unwanted.

The word "cripple" causes a different kind of problem. Originally its dictionary meaning referred to someone who was disabled. Even today that's what most dictionaries will say. The problem with the word is that too often it is used to label a person, as in "He is a cripple." Most people with disabilities don't want a disability to be their only identifying label. They do not like the word at all. Needless to say, words derived from "cripple" and "spastic" like "crip" and "spaz" have no place in the vocabularies of sensitive and loving people.

Why do people have therapy? Why not just wait until the injury heals or accept the body's limits?
Joints need to be moved every day through their full range of movement or they will stiffen. Muscles will grow weak if they are not used. Bones will become brittle and break easily. If the body stays in just one position, wounds called pressure sores will develop. Therapy helps avoid these problems. Most important, it can teach people skills that their bodies would not learn if they were left alone.

How does a prosthesis work?
A prosthesis is designed for each person's needs. A technician makes an impression of the stump and designs the prosthesis to fit. Prosthetic legs and feet often look so much like real ones that people can't tell that they're artificial, especially since they're usually covered with clothing.

An arm or hand prosthesis is usually more obvious. Because the hand's function is so complex, the prosthesis is designed more for what it can do than for how it looks. In fact, with artificial hands, people can develop complex skills such as writing, drawing, driving, holding babies, eating, and playing musical instruments.

Do people who use wheelchairs stay in them all the time?
No. A wheelchair is a way of getting around, like a car or a bike. Unless people need to be kept in wheelchairs for their own safety, they can sit on chairs or couches when they want to. Some people who use wheelchairs can walk, too, but are not able to all the time.

How do people who must use wheelchairs go to the bathroom?
First they find a bathroom that is accessible by wheelchair. This means that there are no steps, the door is wide enough, and the stall is wide and deep enough for a wheelchair. Usually these bathrooms are labeled. Most older stalls are designed so that wheelchairs can move in and stop in front of the toilet. Handrails are mounted on one or both walls to help people get out of their wheelchairs.

Once in the stall, people move forward to use the toilet, often sitting facing the back. Not everyone in a wheelchair uses a toilet this way. It all depends on the person's strength and coordination. Some people need assistance. Learning to use a toilet is often part of a plan that people develop with their therapists.

Is it all right for anyone to park in a handicapped parking space when there are several spaces marked for them and you know no one ever uses them anyway?
No, it's not. It's illegal unless the car's license plate is specially marked or the driver has a card displayed on the dashboard. Think of these places as someone else's driveway. Just because you know your neighbors are probably not going out after midnight does not mean you can park your bike in their driveway. Only people with disabilities have the right to park in places reserved and labeled for them.

What is the difference, if any, between a handicap and a disability?
People often use the words "handicap" and "disability" as if these words mean the same thing, but they really don't.

People with a disability have a physical limitation. There are some things they cannot do. They might not be able to see or hear or walk. Or they might not be able to solve complex problems or control their muscle activity. But most people with disabilities can still do much of what nondisabled people can do if other people let them. A disability can limit or change the way people do things, but it doesn't change or limit what they are.

43

. . . MORE QUESTIONS

Disabilities become handicaps when physical or social barriers prevent people from doing all that they are able to do. For example, people who use a wheelchair are handicapped when they sit at the bottom of just one step to a theater. Blind people are handicapped when they stand at a traffic light that has no clickers or beepers to tell them what the signals are or when an elevator has no Braille numbers to identify the floors. People using crutches or canes are handicapped if snow and ice are not cleared from the sidewalks, streets, and other places where they walk.

Social barriers also turn a person with a disability into a handicapped person. A social barrier is one we set up in our heads. We handicap people with disabilities when we let ourselves think that they would rather be taken care of than take care of themselves. Social barriers are hard for people with disabilities to get past because they are often erected by people who mean well. We must remember that all people have the right to a life of freedom of choice, dignity, and accomplishment.

THINGS TO DO AND THINK ABOUT

These projects will help you understand more about living with physical disabilities. You'll see how much people are limited not by their own bodies but by conditions other people create.

1. Plan a morning of getting around town. Make a list of all the places you wouldn't have been able to go if you had been in a wheelchair. Note stairs, curbs, toilet stalls, narrow doors and aisles, and anything else that would stop you. Look for curb cuts, elevators, automatic doors, and handicapped parking spaces. If these are available but hard to find, they can be useless.

2. Leave a message for people who illegally park their cars in places reserved for people who have disabilities. You'll know who is legally parked because their car will be marked in one of the following ways: The license plate will display the international symbol of physical disability.

Or the car will have a permit displayed on the dashboard inside the front windshield. Anyone else is illegally parked if the space is marked with a sign next to, above, or on the parking place.

Leave your message on the windshield. Your city or county social service office may already have a pamphlet you can use. If not, make one up. Point out that this space is reserved for people with disabilities and ask the driver to be more thoughtful. You'll probably notice that people usually park illegally when a lot is crowded or weather is bad, just when a disabled person would most need the parking space.

3. Have you ever tried climbing a snowbank on crutches and sliding down the other side to the street? If you live where winter means snow, check how well the snow has been removed from curb ramps and handicapped parking spaces. Would a person in a wheelchair or on crutches be restricted to home until spring where you live?

4. Ask your parents if there were curb cuts when they were kids or if schools built ramps so kids and teachers in wheelchairs could get in. Ask them if reviewers mentioned whether restaurants were accessible by wheelchair or if government buildings had ramps and elevators. Ask them if they saw wheelchairs in theaters or malls. Ask them if they saw wheelchairs anywhere except in hospitals. Then look around you.

Things have changed. Many of the changes came from the hard, patient work of people who were physically disabled but not politically disabled. They are still working because there is still a lot to do. If you want to help, too, check your phone book for a local chapter of one of the groups listed below. Call and ask what you can do as a volunteer worker.

WHERE TO WRITE FOR FURTHER INFORMATION

The people at these organizations will send you free information about living with physical disabilities if you write to them. Some of the organizations have state and local offices as well as the national ones listed here. If they're listed in your phone book, you can give them a call. Some of them offer programs just for children and will send someone to talk to your class or group. Whether you write or call, give your reason for wanting the information so they can send you material that suits your purpose.

American Academy for Cerebral Palsy and
   Developmental Medicine
2315 Westwood Avenue
P.O. Box 11086
Richmond, VA 23230

Easter Seal Society
2023 West Ogden Avenue
Chicago, IL 60612

March of Dimes Birth Defects Foundation
1275 Mamaroneck Avenue
White Plains, NY 10605

National Association of the Physically Handicapped
76 Elm Street
London, OH 43140

National Library Services for the Blind and
   Physically Handicapped
Library of Congress
1291 Taylor Street NW
Washington, DC 20542

National Spinal Cord Injury Association
149 California Street
Newton, MA 02158

National Wheelchair Athletic Association
2107 Templeton Gap Road, Suite C
Colorado Springs, CO 80907

United Cerebral Palsy Associations
66 East 34th Street
New York, NY 10016

MORE BOOKS ABOUT CHILDREN AND PHYSICAL DISABILITIES

The people in the books listed below have physical disabilities. You may be surprised at how much their dreams and feelings are like yours.

Anna Joins In. Arnold (Abingdon)
Karen. Killilea (Dell)
Let the Balloon Go. Southall (Bradbury)
Margaret's Moves. Rabe (Dutton)
Max's Dream. Mayne (Greenwillow)
Nick Joins In. Lasker (Whitman)
Our Teacher's in a Wheelchair. Powers (Whitman)
A Way of His Own. Dyer (Houghton Mifflin)

GLOSSARY

The words listed below will help you learn more about physical disabilities, effects on the body, and their treatment.

acquired disability: a condition that results from an injury or illness, rather than a condition that occurred before birth.

atrophy: to weaken or to waste away to the point of uselessness. This can happen to muscles if they are not used, for example, after an injury.

brain damage: a defect of the brain that prevents a person from doing certain things, like moving, thinking, seeing, or hearing.

congenital disability: a condition a person has from birth that limits the ability to do something.

impairment: loss of strength, feeling, or the ability to move.

multiple disabilities: more than one disability in a person. People with physical disabilities will frequently have more than one.

orthopedic: having to do with the bones, muscles, and joints used in movement.

paralysis: lost or impaired movement, feeling, or strength of a part of the body.

paraplegia: paralysis of the lower part of the body, usually caused by damage to the spinal cord. Messages cannot be sent from the brain to the part of the body that is below the point of damage.

physical disability: a physical impairment that limits a person's activity.

prosthesis: an artificial replacement for a missing body part, such as a hand or a leg.

quadriplegia: a condition of paralysis of the body from the neck down; "quadri" means "four" — all four limbs are affected.

therapy: a method of treating a disease, disorder, disability, or injury. Therapy can include exercise, medication, education, or a combination of these. The purpose of therapy can be to cure the disease or disorder or to increase the person's skills when the condition is permanent.

INDEX